SRA OPEN COURT READING

Magic Pages

A Division of The McGraw·Hill Companies

Columbus, Ohio

www.sra4kids.com

SRA/McGraw-Hill

A Division of The **McGraw·Hill** *Companies*

Copyright © 2002 by SRA/McGraw-Hill.

Printed in the United States of America.

Send all inquiries to:
SRA/McGraw-Hill
8787 Orion Place
Columbus, OH 43240-4027

ISBN 0-07-569739-4
3 4 5 6 7 8 9 DBH 05 04 03 02

When I read magic pages,
I can take a trip.

I can travel to distant places and hunt for gems.

I can swim with sharks.
I can ride on the back of a charging whale.

I can hunt for giant shells
that whisper in my ear.

I can watch camels run
and giraffes stand in the sun.

When the pages end, my magic trip is done.
I am back home in my bed!